Caves

Written by Margaret MacDonald

Picture Dictionary

glacier cave

limestone cave

lava tube cave

sea cave

A cave is a hole
in the Earth's crust.
Long, long ago,
people lived in caves.
Some animals, such as bats,
live in caves.
Some animals, such as bears,
live in caves in winter.

Some caves form in ice.
Some caves form in rock.
Some caves form in cliffs.

Some caves are very big.
They may have many rooms.
They may have tunnels.
They may have rivers.
They may have a high roof.

Some caves are very small.

People can visit this big cave in Malaysia.

Glacier Caves

You can find glacier caves
in glaciers.
In summer, glaciers start to melt.
Water runs through cracks
in the ice.
The water melts more ice.
A big hole forms.
It is called a glacier cave.

A glacier cave in a glacier

Lava Tube Caves

You can find lava tube caves
in the rock around volcanoes.
When a volcano erupts,
hot lava flows down the volcano.
When the hot lava flows
down the volcano,
it starts to cool down.
When the top cools down,
it turns into hard rock.
The hot lava
under the hard rock
flows on.

It leaves a hole under the rock.
The hole is long like a tube.
The hole is called
a lava tube cave.

A lava tube cave in Hawaii

Limestone Caves

You can find limestone caves in soft rock called limestone.

Limestone caves form when rainwater wears away the limestone rock.
Over time, holes and tunnels form in the rock.
These holes and tunnels form caves.
Most of Earth's caves are limestone caves.

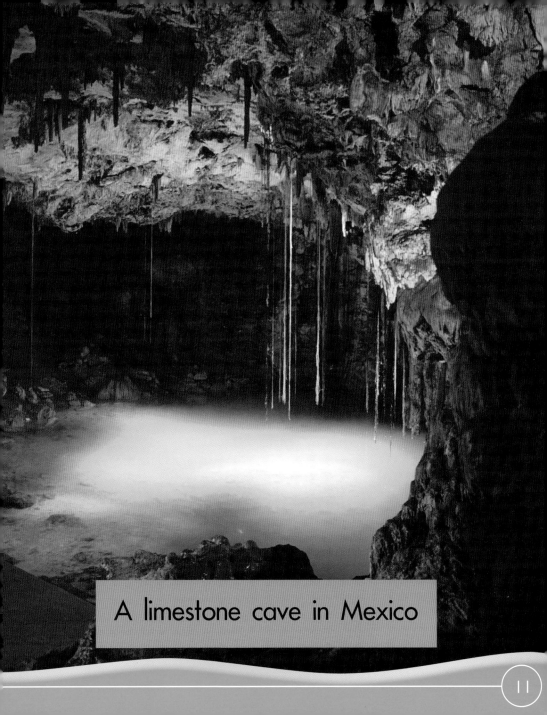

A limestone cave in Mexico

Sea Caves

You can find sea caves in cliffs along rocky coasts of oceans.

Sea caves form when waves crash against rocky cliffs. Over time, the waves wear away the rock. After many years, caves form at the bottom of the cliffs. These caves are called sea caves.

Sea caves in Hawaii

Types of Caves

Glacier cave

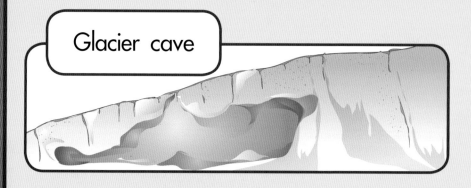

Lava tube cave

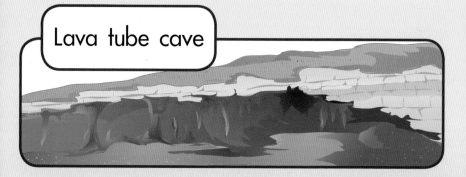

Limestone cave

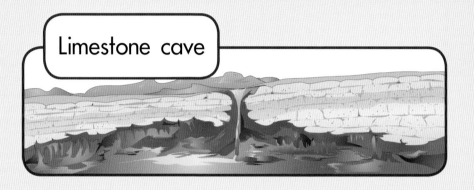

Sea caves

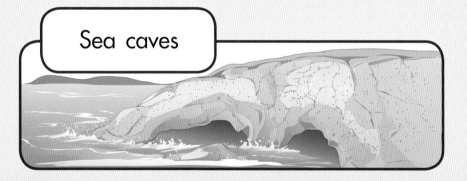

Activity Page

1. Reread the book.

2. Answer the questions.
   - Which caves form in ice?
   - Which caves form in rocky cliffs?
   - Which caves form when rainwater wears away soft rock?
   - Which caves form in the rock around volcanoes?

Do you know the dictionary words?